W9-CHZ-259

WITHDRAWN

My Pet

My Guinea Pig

By Sarah Hughes

Children's Press
A Division of Grolier Publishing
New York / London / Hong Kong / Sydney
Danbury, Connecticut

Photo Credits: Cover, pp. 5, 7, 9, 11, 13, 15, 17, 19, 21 by Maura Boruchow
Contributing Editor: Jeri Cipriano
Book Design: Nelson Sa

Visit Children's Press on the Internet at:
http://publishing.grolier.com

Library of Congress Cataloging-in-Publication Data

Hughes, Sarah.
    My guinea pig / by Sarah Hughes.
      p. cm.—(Hard Work)
    Includes bibliographical references and index.
    ISBN 0-516-23186-3 (lib. bdg.)—ISBN 0-516-23289-4 (pbk.)
    1. Guinea pigs as pets—Juvenile literature.
  [1. Guinea pigs. 2. Pets.] I. Title. II. Series.

 SF459 .G9 H92 2000
 636.9′ 3592—dc21

                                                          00-060100

Copyright © 2001 by Rosen Book Works, Inc.
All rights reserved. Published simultaneously in Canada.
Printed in the United States of America.
    2 3 4 5 6 7 8 9 10 R 05 04 03 02 01

Contents

1 Meet Patti   4

2 Patti Plays   10

3 What Patti Eats   12

4 Petting Patti   20

5 New Words   22

6 To Find Out More   23

7 Index   24

8 About the Author   24

Hi, I'm Rachel.

This is my pet
guinea pig, Patti.

4

5

A guinea pig is not a pig at all.

A guinea pig is a kind of **rodent**.

Mice and squirrels are also rodents.

Patti lives in a cage.

There are toys for Patti
in the cage.

9

Patti likes to play.

She likes to play with balls.

I give Patti food **pellets**.

She also eats green, leafy **vegetables**.

I give Patti water.

Patti drinks from a special **bottle**.

I take Patti out of her cage.

I am very careful.

Every week, I help clean Patti's cage.

I put new paper in the bottom.

I like to pet Patti.

She is soft and warm.

I love my guinea pig.

New Words

bottle (**bot**-l) something that holds a drink

guinea pig (**gin**-ee **pig**) a small, fat animal with short ears

pellets (**pel**-its) little balls of food

rodent (**roh**-dnt) a kind of small animal, with large front teeth

vegetables (**vej**-tuh-bulz) part of a plant eaten as food

To Find Out More

Books
All About Your Guinea Pig
by Bradley Viner
Barrons Educational Series

Becoming Best Friends With Your Hamster, Guinea Pig, or Rabbit
by Bill Gutman
Millbrook Press

Web Sites
Mr. Mischief—Guinea Pigs
http://worldkids.net/critters/mischief/cavies.htm
Find out how to take care of a guinea pig.

The Guinea Pig Club
http://www.petclubhouse.com/guineapig/
Play guinea pig games and learn about famous
people who had guinea pigs as pets.

Index

bottle, 14   pellets, 12   toys, 8

guinea pig,   rodent, 6   vegetables,
  4, 6, 20   12

About the Author
Sarah Hughes taught school for twelve years. She now writes and edits children's books. Sarah lives in New York City and enjoys running and riding her bike.

Reading Consultants
Kris Flynn, Coordinator, Small School District Literacy, The San Diego County Office of Education

Shelly Forys, Certified Reading Recovery Specialist, W.J. Zahnow Elementary School, Waterloo, IL

Peggy McNamara, Professor, Bank Street College of Education, Reading and Literacy Program